THE OFFICIAL
WOLVES
ANNUAL 2021

Written by Paul Berry

Designed by Abbie Groom,
Synaxis Design Consultancy Ltd

A Grange Publication

© 2020. Published by Grange Communications Ltd.,
Edinburgh, under licence from Wolverhampton
Wanderers Football Club. Printed in the EU.

Every effort has been made to ensure the accuracy
of information within this publication but the
publishers cannot be held responsible for any errors
or omissions. Views expressed are those of the
author and do not necessarily represent those of the
publishers or the football club. All rights reserved.

Photographs © AMA Sports Photo Agency -
Sam Bagnall, Matt Ashton, Dave Bagnall,
Robbie Jay Barratt, James Baylis; Stuart Manley
Photography – Stuart Manley, Shaun Mallen;
Simon Faulkner; PA Images and the Wolves Archive.

ISBN: 978-1-913578-09-1

We hope you
enjoy this year's Annual.
Due to the extension of the
summer transfer window because
of COVID-19, we had to print this
edition before the window closed.
There may, therefore, be some features
or players that are not as up-to-date
as we would like them to be. We
appreciate your understanding
of this, and your continued
loyalty, in difficult times.

PIX

FROM THE PACK:

THE PORTUGUESE PROTECTOR

RUI PATRICIO

GOALKEEPER

Contents

NUNO HAD A DREAM

Thanks to Fin Morris for his 'Nuno Had a Dream' page design!

It has been an incredible first three seasons for Nuno Espirito Santo and his backroom staff at Wolves.

The Championship title, successive seventh-placed Premier League finishes, an FA Cup semi-final and a Europa League quarter-final all featured in an exciting trio of campaigns.

With the number of fixtures Wolves had to play during the 2019/20 season, Nuno's games in charge surged past the 150 mark, during which he registered the highest ever win percentage – over 50 per cent - of any Molineux manager.

Here, the Wolves Annual looks back at just five highlights from so many memorable matches, and moments, so far in Nuno's reign.

06/04/2018
PENALTY POWER AT CARDIFF

The game that had everything.

A fantastic Ruben Neves free kick, mounting tension as the final whistle approached, and then not one, but two Cardiff penalties in time added on.

John Ruddy saved from Gary Madine and then Junior Hoilett shot over, sparking wild scenes of celebration among the travelling faithful and a slight disagreement between Nuno and Neil Warnock as Wolves clung on.

Above all else, this was a sign of how Nuno and Wolves had learnt from life in the Championship, recovering from being outmuscled by Cardiff earlier in the campaign to register the win which took them nine points clear at the top of the table.

05/12/2018
CHANGING IT UP FOR CHELSEA

Wolves' return to the Premier League for 2018/19 had gone through something of an up-and-down start, but by the time Chelsea arrived in early December, they were struggling.

The team had picked up just one point out of a possible 18, despite still producing decent performances against the likes of Tottenham and Arsenal, and that is why there was no reaching for the panic button.

Whilst both meticulous and almost metronomic in his work with players on the training pitch particularly around shape both in and out of possession, Nuno has always shown he is ready to change tactics if required.

He changed Wolves' normal formation to a 3-5-2, pairing Raul Jimenez and Diogo Jota together (both scored), utilising Morgan Gibbs-White as a number ten (he had a stormer) and watching on as his team hit back to post a famous 2-1 victory.

And that, in the process, prompted a change in Wolves' fortunes which saw them win three on the bounce and seven out of 11 in the Premier League.

16/03/2019
MAJESTIC AGAINST MANCHESTER UTD

For one of the most electric atmospheres at Molineux in recent years, look no further than the night Wolves welcomed Manchester United on a Saturday evening in March for an FA Cup quarter-final.

Thrillingly tense, the game was locked at stalemate until Raul Jimenez struck in the 70th minute before the roof was lifted off the stadium when Diogo Jota broke clear to smash the ball home six minutes later. United grabbed a late consolation but it was Wolves who prevailed to continue a thrilling FA Cup run which had already seen them beat Liverpool and just about survive against Shrewsbury Town.

It was another night where Nuno was lauded for his tactics and the performance of the team, which booked a first FA Cup semi-final in 21 years. It was also another game where Wolves were now showing they could match, and better, some of the top names in English football, even amid the pressure and profile surrounding such an intense FA Cup assignment.

03/10/2019
BOLY BULLIES BESIKTAS

Nuno has also masterminded Wolves' return to proper European competition for the first time in almost four decades.

There were so many highlights in the run to the Europa League quarter-finals – and fans may cite the win at Torino for its atmosphere – but it is another away tie which showed Wolves had properly arrived at this level.

Having lost their first group game to Braga, Wolves were back on the road to take on Turkish giants Besiktas, famed for their intimidating atmosphere which had previously seen off both Tottenham and Liverpool in Istanbul.

Wolves produced a composed and accomplished performance to nullify that atmosphere and nullify their opponents, before starting to turn the screw in the second half. And with just seconds of added time remaining, the big man from the back Willy Boly, calmly controlled the ball and tucked it home following a set piece to secure a famous victory which had Wolves up and running in the group.

27/12/2019
JUST WHAT THE DOC ORDERED

Wolves had already defeated reigning champions Manchester City at the Etihad Stadium earlier in the season, just three days after that Besiktas triumph, and Pep Guardiola's team arrived at Molineux towards the end of 2019 in desperate need of three points to maintain their pursuit of Liverpool. What an incredible night it proved to be.

City keeper Ederson was sent off early on after cleaning out Jota, but the visitors still worked their way into a two-goal lead thanks to a brace from Raheem Sterling – the first from the rebound after a twice-taken penalty was again saved by Rui Patricio. Wolves weren't to be denied however, with Adama Traore firing home not long after Sterling's second and then setting up Jimenez to level things up with just eight minutes remaining. The winning goal, a minute from time, was a thing of beauty, Matt Doherty heavily involved in a flowing move which finished with him cutting inside and expertly drilling a left-foot shot into the bottom corner.

"I cannot lie, when I started, we didn't know what was in front of us, but what we knew was that we had a fantastic club to take care of and try to become as huge as it was in its past history."

JULY
2019

It was a very rare July of competitive action for Wolves, with seventh place in the previous season enough to have secured a spot in the Europa League qualifying rounds.

And so, on July 25th, Wolves welcomed Crusaders from the Northern Ireland Premiership to Molineux, for a second qualifying round tie played out in front of a crowd of 29,708.

Ignoring the club's participation in the Anglo-Italian Cup, this was Wolves' first European tie at Molineux since taking on PSV Eindhoven all the way back in 1980, and it would be a winning return against what was a hard-working Crusaders side.

Diogo Jota became the first Wolves player to score in a European tie since Mel Eves by breaking the deadlock on 37 minutes, before Ruben Vinagre secured a 2-0 victory in added time.

Having said that, Wolves had already made one successful trip overseas even before kicking off their European adventure, thanks to a successful first ever participation in the Asia Trophy.

A 4-0 semi-final win against Newcastle in Nanjing was followed by victory on penalties against reigning Premier League champions Manchester City in the final in Shanghai, Rui Patricio saving three spot kicks in the shoot-out after a goalless draw, with Raheem Sterling having blazed a penalty over the bar in the 90 minutes.

MOMENT
OF THE MONTH:

Diogo Jota scoring the first goal of Wolves' season, and the first in top European competition for almost 40 years.

W   W   D   W   D   W   D   W

AUGUST
2019

There was no easing into the new season as sometimes happens in August, with Wolves playing no fewer than eight fixtures in what is normally the traditional opening month of the campaign.

The Premier League curtain-raiser at Leicester saw the first of many VAR-related controversies to follow as Leander Dendoncker's goal was ruled out after the ball struck Willy Boly's arm at close range.

The game finished goalless, and Wolves would also draw their first two home league games, this time 1-1, coming from behind on both occasions.

A spectacular Ruben Neves strike levelled matters against Manchester United, after which Rui Patricio saved Paul Pogba's penalty, but Raul Jimenez made no mistake from the spot with an equaliser in the seventh minute of added time against Burnley.

It was in the Europa League where Wolves made significant progress, overcoming Crusaders 4-1 in their second leg before winning 4-0 both home and away against Pyunik in the third qualifying round.

That set up a magnificent night in Turin as Wolves won 3-2 against Torino, before prevailing 2-1 at Molineux to secure a place in the group stages.

MOMENT OF THE MONTH:

Very difficult to ignore the Neves superstrike but Wolves' night in Turin was special, as was Raul Jimenez's fantastic solo effort for the third goal.

SEPTEMBER
2019

Having started the Premier League with three draws, things didn't initially improve for Wolves during September, with some uncharacteristically lax defending seeing the month start with a 3-2 reverse at Everton followed up with a 5-2 defeat at home to Chelsea.

Another of many late Wolves goals during the season was to prove something of a turning point, as Diogo Jota pounced five minutes into added time to secure a 1-1 draw at Crystal Palace.

And that result paved the way for a first league win of the campaign, goals in either half, from Matt Doherty and an own goal, making for a comfortable victory at home to Watford.

Wolves had won six out of six in the Europa League, in contrast to that league start, although the group stages didn't follow suit with a 1-0 defeat at home to Braga the only fixture in the competition played during the month.

There was progress in the EFL Cup, albeit the hard way, beating Reading 4-2 on penalties after conceding a 99th-minute equaliser at Molineux.

MOMENT OF THE MONTH:

Has to be Jota again, given the previous two league results, for that equaliser at Palace which launched a run of 11 unbeaten in the league.

OCTOBER

2019

Three league games in October and the highlight undoubtedly came with the first.

A trip to the Etihad Stadium saw Wolves win at the venue for the first time, and indeed the first time away to Manchester City in the top flight since 1979.

Adama Traore was the hero with two clinical finishes to round off superb breakaways, but overall it was a fantastic team performance which also saw several other Wolves chances spurned.

By now Wolves were already almost 20 games into their season such were their Europa League exploits, but there was nothing wrong with

their mentality, coming from behind to secure 1-1 draws at home to Southampton and away at Newcastle.

And the two Europa trips in the month both ended in success, Willy Boly notching an added-time winner at Besiktas and Romain Saiss and Raul Jimenez (penalty) helping the team come from behind to win 2-1 at Slovan Bratislava.

Wolves did exit one competition in October, as Nuno shuffled his pack and a very youthful team including four Academy debutants – one of whom, Chem Campbell, was just 16 – were beaten 2-1 at Aston Villa in the EFL Cup.

MOMENT OF THE MONTH:

Has to be that incredible victory at Manchester City, sealed by some fantastic scenes in front of the travelling fans following Adama Traore's second goal.

NOVEMBER
2019

November has sometimes not been a happy hunting ground for Wolves in recent years, but there was no problem on this occasion, as the 2019 vintage recorded an unbeaten five games in domestic and European competition.

The first Premier League game saw Wolves post a third successive 1-1 draw, this one at Arsenal, before a 2-1 home win against Aston Villa that was perhaps more comfortable than the result suggests and victory at Bournemouth by the same scoreline.

In Europe, the group stages continued with a narrow win at home to Slovan Bratislava thanks to yet another added-time goal, Raul Jimenez on target after Ruben Neves' earlier penalty had been saved.

A thrilling 3-3 draw away in Braga was then enough for both sides to secure qualification from Group K.

Goals from Jimenez, Matt Doherty and Adama Traore helped Wolves secure a share of the spoils, meaning all that was left to decide from the outstanding fixture was who would win the group and who would progress as runners-up.

MOMENT OF THE MONTH:

Local derbies with Aston Villa have become spicy encounters in recent years and Ruben Neves' superb opener from a cheeky free-kick routine was well worth the occasion!

DECEMBER
2019

The usual packed programme for December with Wolves coming through seven Premier League fixtures and one in the Europa League, in which a 4-0 home win against Besiktas wasn't enough to claim top spot in the group with Braga also collecting three points elsewhere.

It did, however, signal one of the quickest hat-tricks in Europa League history as Diogo Jota came off the bench to bag a treble in 12 second-half minutes.

The first treble of the month in terms of league fixtures saw Wolves continue their mix of wins and draws, stalemates against Sheffield United and Brighton sandwiching a comfortable home success against West Ham.

The visit of Jose Mourinho's Tottenham brought an end to Wolves'

11-game unbeaten league run, but only thanks to an added-time goal from Jan Vertonghen, and, as so often, Nuno's team responded impressively by taking all three points from Norwich at Carrow Road.

That teed up a mouth-watering finale to 2019 with fixtures against the top two, and if the year was to finish with a controversial and narrow 1-0 defeat at Liverpool, by then Wolves had already enjoyed another fantastic result in completing the league double over champions Manchester City.

City's keeper Ederson was sent off early on, but a Raheem Sterling brace, the first from a twice-taken penalty that was saved, put the visitors in charge before goals from Adama Traore, Raul Jimenez and Matt Doherty – in the 89th minute – sealed a famous win.

MOMENT OF THE MONTH:

It can only be that incredible win against Manchester City, and in particular Matt Doherty's superb late goal which earned Wolves the double against the reigning champions. And he even smiled!

13

L D D L W L

JANUARY
2020

The launchpad to 2020 wasn't the best for Wolves, a rare below-par performance finishing in a 2-1 defeat to Watford at Vicarage Road.

A 1-1 draw against Newcastle at Molineux followed, and then finding themselves 2-0 adrift at half time at Southampton, all of a sudden there was the sniff of a crisis.

So often with this Wolves team though, as soon as the alarm bells ring, they are immediately answered in emphatic style, and a magnificent second-half comeback ensued thanks to goals from Pedro Neto and a Raul Jimenez brace.

Wolves then showed they were back in the groove by pushing runaway Premier League winners Liverpool all the way at Molineux, a sumptuous Jimenez header from Adama Traore's cross cancelling out Jordan Henderson's early opener.

Unfortunately, Roberto Firmino was to pop up six minutes from time to secure Liverpool a result they perhaps didn't deserve, but Wolves were once again looking in the mood.

They had, however, exited the FA Cup after the first two meetings of a quickfire trilogy with Manchester United, Juan Mata notching the only goal of the game in the Third Round replay at Old Trafford after the scorers weren't troubled at Molineux.

MOMENT OF THE MONTH:

Moments of the month plural perhaps, with that fantastic second-half comeback at St Mary's, finished off by Jimenez, courtesy of yet another assist from Traore.

D D W W L

FEBRUARY
2020

February was to prove a miserly month at Molineux, in the sense that Wolves did not concede a single goal in their trio of Premier League assignments.

The third instalment in a growing rivalry with Manchester United finished in the same way as three of their four meetings during the season, as a draw, and Valentine's Day brought an identical 0-0 result at home to Leicester.

It was also the same result as hunted from the Foxes on the season's opening day, including a similar VAR controversy to boot, Willy Boly's header ruled out after Pedro Neto was judged offside in the build-up.

Wolves returned to the goal charts in some style towards the end of the month, dispatching Norwich 3-0 in the league on the back of a 4-0 victory against Espanyol in which Diogo Jota bagged his second successive Europa League hat-trick.

The second leg of the round-of-32 tie thus became something of a procession, and a 3-2 defeat to the La Liga side did nothing to dent more significant progress as Wolves moved deep into the competition.

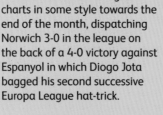

MOMENT OF THE MONTH:

Shared between Diogo Jota, for another European hat-trick, and Ruben Neves, for a typically spectacular strike in the same game against Espanyol.

MARCH
2020

March was the month when football – and indeed the world as a whole – came to a standstill as the Covid-19 global pandemic took hold.

Wolves played two games in the Premier League prior to the season being delayed, and the first was a particular cracker.

Heading to face Tottenham, who they had overcome at Wembley in the corresponding fixture the previous season, twice Wolves fell behind and twice they hit back to equalise through Matt Doherty and Diogo Jota.

And then it was that man Raul Jimenez once again, clinically dispatching the winner 17 minutes from time.

Wolves couldn't follow up with a win at home to a stubborn Brighton side who held on for a goalless draw before the final game before lockdown, the first leg of the Europa League last-16 tie away in Olympiacos.

The game was played behind closed doors due to the pandemic, and the halting of the Premier League was announced not long after full time, by which point Wolves had secured a 1-1 draw against their ten-man opponents thanks to Pedro Neto's second-half goal.

MOMENT OF THE MONTH:

Another comeback, another late winner, and Wolves take all three points from Tottenham, with Raul Jimenez the man yet again notching the vital goal.

JUNE
2020

With football returning behind closed doors, Wolves travelled to West Ham, a fixture originally postponed three days before it was due to take place, and now signalling a return to action for Nuno's team some 100 days after their Europa League trip to Olympiacos.

Despite that lengthy absence, and despite missing the normal and raucous travelling support, Wolves were straight back to their best against the Hammers, Raul Jimenez heading home a cross from – you guessed it – Adama Traore, before Pedro Neto almost burst the net with a sweetly struck volley.

The games were coming thick and fast for the Premier League restart – three in eight days – but Wolves seemed to revel in the schedule, particularly with the defence looking so solid and well organised.

Next up came the visit of Bournemouth to Molineux, Jimenez heading home Traore's cross on the hour mark, before the month finished with the return of the Midlands derby and a trip to Villa Park.

Again it was 0-0 at half time, and again Wolves kept a clean sheet, their seventh in eight league games, and this time it was the reliably versatile Leander Dendoncker who popped up with a neat second-half finish to seal the win.

MOMENT OF THE MONTH:

Not a hint of rustiness for Pedro Neto, who, within 20 minutes of coming off the bench, fires home an exquisite left-foot volley against West Ham. A hammer blow you might say!

17

L L W D W L

JULY
2020

Just the six games in 23 days in July to finish off this most extraordinary of seasons, and Wolves began the month, buoyed by three consecutive wins since the restart, with genuine aspirations of making the top four and Champions League.

Unfortunately, however, back-to-back defeats in very different circumstances at the start of the month were to make that dream appear very unlikely.

Wolves found Arsenal too difficult an opposition at Molineux in falling to a 2-0 defeat but had ground out what appeared to be a decent point at Sheffield

United only for the Blades to notch the latest of winners.

Wolves, as ever, responded well with successive and comfortable home wins against Everton and Crystal Palace, but another cruel blow was sandwiched in between with a controversial late penalty for Burnley allowing them to snatch a 1-1 draw at Turf Moor.

That left Wolves needing to win at Chelsea on the final day to guarantee sixth position and a Europa League spot, but the hosts proved too strong leaving Nuno's stoic squad posting what was still a very impressive seventh-placed finish.

MOMENT OF THE MONTH:

Sadly it wasn't to prove the game's decisive moment but Raul Jimenez's superb goal against Burnley was certainly one for the memory bank.

AUGUST
2020

And so on to August, not for the start of the new season, but still the finish, well the European finish, of the previous one.

The Europa League, delayed by the pandemic, was to be played out to its conclusion, starting with the second leg at home to Olympiacos, a mere 147 days after the 1-1 draw behind closed doors in Greece.

It was a nervy night at Molineux, but Raul Jimenez's early penalty – coupled with some fine defending and a couple of vital saves from Rui Patricio - proved to be sufficient to take Wolves through to the quarter-finals.

The last eight onwards was to be played on a knockout basis, over in Germany, and this is where

it got particularly serious, with Wolves facing five-times previous winners Sevilla.

Again there was the award of an early penalty thanks to an incredible run from Adama Traore, but agonisingly – and so rarely – Jimenez saw his effort saved, and after a tense contest, which the Spanish side largely controlled, they struck a cruel blow with the winning goal just two minutes from time.

It was a sad end to such an incredible run which had taken in 17 Europa League fixtures, and indeed an incredible season as a whole.

Fifty-nine games played across 383 days in ten different countries. Very much a marathon not a sprint!

MOMENT OF THE MONTH:
Powerful pictures after the victory against Olympiacos as Nuno called his players and staff together for a huddle and message of support in front of an empty Molineux.

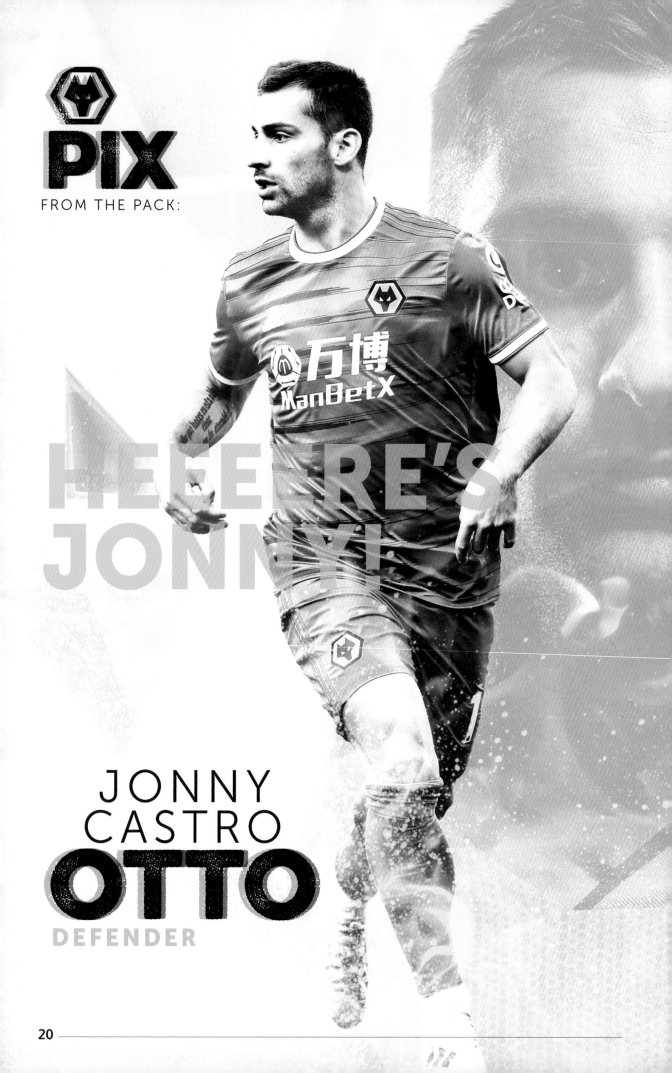

PIX
FROM THE PACK:

HEEERE'S
JONNY!

JONNY
CASTRO
OTTO
DEFENDER

WOLVES IN EUROPE!

"WE'RE ALL GOING ON A EUROPEAN TOUR"
SANG THE WOLVES FANS REPEATEDLY.
SO MANY GAMES. SO MANY MILES.
NOT FAR SHY OF 20,000 IN FACT! AND SO MANY MEMORIES.

The previous pages carried details of those 17 Europa League fixtures which dipped in and out of Wolves' season en route to the quarter-finals in Germany, some 13 months after kicking off the campaign against Crusaders.

It was the club's first foray into top European competition for four decades, and their performance was the best on the continent since the class of 1971/72 were beaten in the final of the very first UEFA Cup tournament by Tottenham.

Thanks to photographers Matt Ashton, Sam Bagnall and Robbie Jay Barratt, on the next few pages we carry some of the more stadium-based and supporter photos, highlighting a fantastic Europa League journey which captured the hearts of the Molineux faithful.

V

COUNTRY:
Northern Ireland

THE ROUND:
Second Qualifying Round

HOW FAR AWAY?
416 miles round trip

AND IN SHORT...
Raul Jimenez at the double helping Wolves to a comfortable 4-1 win to seal a 6-1 aggregate success, although the Crusaders actually notched first in what was Nuno's 100th game in charge.

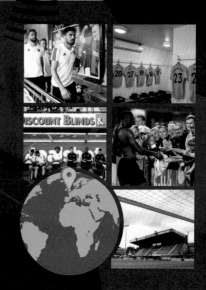

DATELINE:
01/08/19

OPPOSITION:
CRUSADERS

 V

COUNTRY:
Armenia

THE ROUND:
Third Qualifying Round

HOW FAR AWAY?
4868 miles round trip

AND IN SHORT...
Another Jimenez brace as Wolves bag four on their travels once again, this time without reply, ahead of rattling up the same scoreline in the second leg which followed.

DATELINE:
08/08/19

OPPOSITION:
FC PYUNIK

 V

COUNTRY:
Italy

THE ROUND:
Play-Off

HOW FAR AWAY?
1366 miles round trip

AND IN SHORT...
A memorable 3-2 first-leg victory crowning the perfect Italian Job on a night lauded as one of the finest Wolves away days of recent history.

DATELINE:
22/08/19

OPPOSITION:
TORINO

V

COUNTRY:
Turkey

THE ROUND:
Group Stage Matchday 2

HOW FAR AWAY?
3310 miles round trip

DATELINE:
03/10/19

OPPOSITION:
BESIKTAS

AND IN SHORT...
Matchday 2 of the group stage
and the late Boly show as defender
Willy calmly slots home a 93rd-
minute winner, the only goal
of the game. Turkish delight!

 V

COUNTRY:
Slovakia

THE ROUND:
Group Stage Matchday 3

HOW FAR AWAY?
1896 miles round trip

DATELINE:
24/10/19

OPPOSITION:
SLOVAN
BRATISLAVA

AND IN SHORT...
A game supposedly played
behind closed doors sees a stirring
fightback and quickfire goals
from Romain Saiss and Jimenez
secure a 2-1 win and move Wolves
into second place in the group.

 V

COUNTRY:
Portugal

THE ROUND:
Group Stage Matchday 5

HOW FAR AWAY?
1634 miles round trip

DATELINE:
28/11/19

OPPOSITION:
BRAGA

AND IN SHORT...
An exciting encounter sees the
group's top two share six goals
and the silver lining to losing
a 3-1 lead was that the point
was enough to secure progress
to the knockout stages.

COUNTRY:
Spain

THE ROUND:
Last 32

HOW FAR AWAY?
1598 miles round trip

AND IN SHORT...
The Diogo Jota-inspired 4-0 win in the first leg had made this trip a formality, and a late penalty saw Wolves fall to a 3-2 defeat, which was certainly not enough to dampen the delight of the prospect of a last-16 tie to come.

DATELINE:
27/02/20

OPPOSITION:
RCD ESPANYOL

COUNTRY:
Greece

THE ROUND:
Last 16

HOW FAR AWAY?
3198 miles round trip

AND IN SHORT...
Coronavirus concerns saw this game played behind closed doors just before football locked down and Pedro Neto's equaliser in a 1-1 draw provided the crucial away goal to help set up Wolves' progress in the second leg just 147 days later.

DATELINE:
12/03/20

OPPOSITION:
OLYMPIACOS

COUNTRY:
Germany (Neutral)

THE ROUND:
Quarter-Finals

HOW FAR AWAY?
978 miles round trip

AND IN SHORT...
A cruel end to an incredible European journey as Raul Jimenez misses an early penalty and Wolves' battling resistance is only broken two minutes from time by the competition champions Sevilla.

DATELINE:
12/08/20

OPPOSITION:
SEVILLA

PACE
AND
POISE

RUBEN
VINAGRE
DEFENDER

fan-tastic!

It's been another memorable season for Wolves, and certainly for their supporters, whilst they were still able to head to Molineux and other Premier League and European stadia to enjoy seeing their team in action.

Here, is another great collection of fan photos from Molineux during the season, snapped by Stuart Manley Photography.

[STUART**MANLEY**]

SAISS
SAISS
BABY

ROMAIN
SAISS
DEFENDER/MIDFIELDER

MONSTER WORDSEARCH

It's time for this year's Monster Wordsearch, and this is also a tribute to the players who led Wolves in such a fantastic 2019/20 season, which was definitely a marathon and not a sprint!

Hidden inside the grid are the 21 – just 21 – players who Wolves used in the Premier League in the 2019/2020 season and who put in such a magnificent effort to achieve a second successive seventh-placed finish. And, in tribute to the man who masterminded another great season at Molineux, we have sneaked Nuno in as well!

- ☑ BENNETT
- ☑ BOLY
- ☑ COADY
- ☑ CUTRONE
- ☑ DENDONCKER
- ☑ DOHERTY
- ☑ GIBBS-WHITE
- ☑ JIMENEZ
- ☑ JONNY
- ☑ JORDAO
- ☑ JOTA
- ☑ KILMAN
- ☑ MOUTINHO
- ☑ NETO
- ☑ NEVES
- ☑ NUNO
- ☑ PATRICIO
- ☑ PODENCE
- ☑ SAISS
- ☑ TRAORE
- ☑ VALLEJO
- ☑ VINAGRE

Answers on page 61.

O	J	B	A	R	K	B	O	V	I	S	S	A	I	S	S	S	A	A	I	S	B	A	B	Y	O
N	M	O	D	L	K	O	T	I	G	R	A	Y	R	I	C	H	A	C	R	D	B	U	L	L	A
E	I	V	E	E	R	L	P	N	T	R	T	Y	U	T	R	T	U	T	Y	D	C	S	H	L	J
V	N	N	A	W	N	E	L	E	J	O	D	O	H	R	E	T	Y	V	A	L	L	E	G	O	F
E	E	U	R	L	S	Y	O	G	I	U	O	B	O	R	R	O	V	P	S	P	K	A	E	N	W
S	Z	N	S	K	L	D	W	A	M	D	C	R	O	O	L	O	E	A	S	O	I	G	W	G	G
L	J	L	T	R	F	E	E	R	E	F	F	A	M	A	D	N	E	T	B	D	M	U	O	T	A
A	T	I	Q	U	G	R	R	T	N	D	R	E	O	R	O	P	D	R	O	E	L	L	N	R	N
R	O	A	L	D	O	I	C	I	R	T	A	P	U	R	N	A	F	I	S	N	A	L	M	E	E
T	A	M	P	D	R	T	O	R	L	G	P	S	U	D	V	T	I	S	C	N	S	Y	J	R	R
Y	T	N	U	R	F	C	A	A	D	R	E	U	I	D	E	I	A	C	R	E	B	T	S	O	A
H	T	E	H	T	G	O	D	B	J	T	C	O	A	D	Y	N	H	L	T	D	E	A	O	N	J
F	E	T	G	G	F	A	U	I	P	R	O	T	R	E	E	A	U	O	L	E	N	N	N	N	O
W	N	T	D	T	R	D	M	R	R	E	D	L	E	R	A	N	R	B	E	E	N	D	R	Y	L
E	N	O	F	E	T	F	O	O	O	A	D	V	D	T	M	G	D	K	A	R	J	I	T	M	D
F	E	R	D	R	N	Y	U	T	U	T	Y	E	I	H	A	R	W	O	N	W	E	O	A	A	B
G	B	E	S	E	E	C	T	J	O	T	A	R	Y	N	U	N	O	T	N	E	T	O	E	L	O
H	R	D	Z	L	U	U	I	S	R	E	I	T	W	O	A	E	A	R	D	C	T	R	D	L	S
J	S	G	O	P	O	T	N	F	T	D	L	N	O	R	R	G	L	E	E	A	K	P	L	E	T
Y	G	I	B	B	S	W	H	I	T	E	T	O	H	B	J	O	R	D	A	O	P	E	A	N	A
S	I	J	G	Q	M	R	A	B	A	R	R	C	L	O	T	O	E	E	R	R	L	T	R	E	B
T	B	A	T	U	U	T	E	T	B	T	E	G	E	R	S	T	T	E	T	T	D	D	E	V	
E	B	C	Y	E	T	F	Y	D	O	H	E	R	T	Y	G	B	O	T	O	E	I	D	O	J	E
F	S	K	G	E	C	G	T	N	L	O	S	B	R	R	R	T	Y	Y	A	J	O	T	O	O	S
L	W	H	U	N	H	C	R	O	Y	O	T	A	K	I	L	M	A	N	B	G	H	J	K	B	F
T	O	O	X	Y	S	I	T	L	W	P	S	R	A	O	M	N	R	J	R	C	B	Q	W	O	C

SUPPORTING THE COMMUNITY

The arrival of the Covid-19 pandemic provided a major crisis, both physically and mentally, across the entire world. In Wolverhampton, the Wolves family teamed up to try to provide as much support as possible to the local community, in many different ways. Wolves' first-team staff and players made a six-figure donation to help the Royal Wolverhampton NHS Trust increase their capacity. The squad also supported the Premier League's 'Players Together' fund for the NHS and Wolves Foundation distributed a huge amount of PPE equipment such as masks and coveralls – donated by owners Fosun - to local hospitals and care workers. The Foundation also adapted its own projects to continue to deliver online support to schools and other participants, led on the 'Wolves at Home' scheme to phone elderly/ vulnerable supporters and handed over the Arena at Aldersley for the council's food delivery programme. Meanwhile, Foundation Ambassador Karl Henry spearheaded a campaign involving former players and staff and the club's supporters to raise more than £50,000 for New Cross Hospital. Here, are just a few photos of the overall team effort to support those who needed it most during such a difficult time.

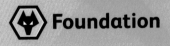

OOH
BOLY
BOLY

WILLY
BOLY
DEFENDER

CAPTAIN COADY!

Conor Coady. Captain Fantastic. Wanderers through and through. What a few years he has had!

Since arriving at Wolves in 2015, the affable Coady's trajectory has grown and grown, not just with his performances on the pitch but his influence off it as Nuno's lieutenant, the man with the armband.

He played every minute of every single Premier League and Europa game in 2019/20, off the back of playing every minute of every game in all competitions the previous year.

Not just Captain Fantastic, but Captain Invincible!

Here, the main man chats about an extraordinary season, and what it still means to him to lead Wolves out as they tackle all-comers at home and abroad.

CONOR, WHAT A UNIQUE SEASON IT WAS IN 2019/20. HOW DO YOU SUM IT UP?

CC: It has been amazing. It's something we didn't expect at the start of the season when you think back to starting out and it being 13 months later that we finished. You don't think you are going to have to keep going for over a year. I think we adapted to the situation we faced because we had to – like everybody in the world, we had to adapt to what was happening. All of a sudden everything stopped because of something horrible that was happening in the world.

WHAT WAS IT LIKE DURING THAT TIME THAT THE SEASON WAS INTERRUPTED? DID YOU HAVE TO KEEP IN TOUCH WITH EVERYONE AS CAPTAIN?

CC: It wasn't a break like some people imagine. We didn't know when we would play again so we had to stay fit in case they said 'we're back next week'. I've got three boys and my wife Amie and I tried to get into a routine with the kids. We tried to do home-schooling with my eldest, Henri, as well as the Joe Wicks online PE classes every morning to keep him active. The staff at Wolves were great in keeping us informed through everything and then putting us in the best possible position when we did restart. As captain, I will always be there to speak to the lads if they need to ask me a question or know where to come. I'm also there to be that little bit of a bridge in terms of whether the manager or people at the higher end of the club want to get things to the boys, so they know they can come through me as well. I am there to pass on messages to whoever I have to.

DOES SOMETHING LIKE THIS MAKE YOU CLOSER IN WHAT IS QUITE A SMALL SQUAD COMPARED TO OTHERS?

CC: I don't think it makes any difference because we don't know anything apart from having a really close squad. Everyone gets on really well. When players come in, we are quick to welcome them and make them feel at home. They adapt to the English game and English culture because they are here to help us and we want them to make a difference for us. We love to play football matches and I think if it was up to us we'd play Saturday-Wednesday-Saturday-Wednesday all the time! We want to play as many games as possible and with a small squad we get to do that.

AND YOU DID HAVE TO PLAY A LOT OF GAMES, 59 IN TOTAL. THE NEW DEVELOPMENT WAS THE EUROPA LEAGUE. HOW DID YOU FIND THAT?

CC: I've loved every part of the competition – it was amazing. And I take a lot of pride in how our club has gone about it this year. We could've gone about it in different ways, but we took it in our stride. We said from the start we didn't want to make up the numbers. We got to the last eight, which is an incredible achievement for a team that was in the Championship three years ago. We said we wanted to do something special, and we were very nearly there. But it wasn't meant to be. We're absolutely gutted. How many games did you say, 59? We still took Sevilla all the way. We're gutted, but it's an amazing achievement.

YOU MENTION THREE YEARS AGO – IT HAS BEEN QUITE A JOURNEY SO FAR?

CC: It was a totally different football club three years ago. A lot of credit has to go to the owners since they came in, who have always been open about what they wanted to do and how they wanted to improve the club. That's what we all want – to improve the club and move it forward. The manager came in and he and his staff changed the direction of the club and I can't praise them enough for getting us to where we are after three years. We want to keep on going now, and keep on making sure this football club is improving. That is the main thing, we have a game-by-game mentality and never think too far ahead, but that is what is helping us enjoy some success and keep getting better.

AS CAPTAIN YOU ARE AT THE CENTRE OF EVERYTHING GOING ON AROUND THE DRESSING ROOM. WHAT DO YOU THINK THE REST OF THE TEAM THINK OF YOU?

CC: They probably think that I am annoying! I am quite loud and wind people up a little bit. I also hope they would say I am quite helpful and am there to speak to when needed. I love playing here and playing with this team and whatever they say about me it's no problem!

YOU'VE TOUCHED ON IT THERE, BUT, FINALLY, WHAT DOES IT MEAN FOR YOU TO BE WOLVES CAPTAIN?

CC: The pride I have leading this club, walking out with this football club every single game, is immense. It's something I live for. I love playing for this football club, so to do it so many times is amazing. Hopefully, I can keep on going.

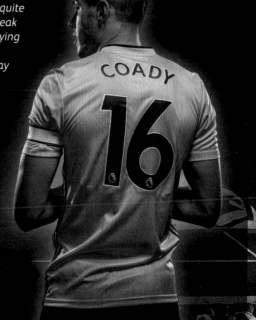

QUIZ:
TWENTY'S PLENTY!

So it's time for another quiz, and taking in the first 20 years of the new millennium, this one's called 'Guess the Year'.

We provide details of an event or match which took place between 2000 and 2020, and give you several options to try and pick out the correct year. It's been quite a couple of decades!

1 Molineux is rocking for the second leg of a play-off semi-final as Wolves try and overturn a 3-1 defeat at Norwich. A Kevin Cooper goal secures a 1-0 win, but it's not enough.
- A 2001
- B 2002
- C 2003

6 Benik Afobe comes off the bench to score on his first Wolves debut against Blackpool.
- A 2015
- B 2016
- C 2017

2 Wolves make a club record signing with the arrival of striker Kevin Doyle from Reading for £6.5 million.
- A 2009
- B 2010
- C 2011

7 Wolves draw 1-1 at home to Plymouth, making it their fifth successive 1-1 draw in the Championship.
- A 2004
- B 2005
- C 2006

3 Dave Edwards departs Wolves after nine-and-a-half years at Molineux after making 307 appearances and scoring 44 goals.
- A 2016
- B 2017
- C 2018

8 Wolves win 1-0 at Cardiff with the home side squandering two chances to equalise from the penalty spot in added time.
- A 2016
- B 2017
- C 2018

4 The versatile Neil Emblen leaves Wolves after his second stint at the club, signing for Norwich City.
- A 2000
- B 2001
- C 2002

9 Paul Ince scores in a 4-2 win against his former club West Ham United and celebrates by running in front of the lower tier of the Steve Bull Stand.
- A 2003
- B 2004
- C 2005

5 Goals from George Elokobi and Kevin Doyle help Wolves to a famous Molineux win and end Manchester United's season-long unbeaten league record.
- A 2009
- B 2010
- C 2011

10 Sylvan Ebanks-Blake scores his 50th Wolves goal.
- A 2011
- B 2012
- C 2013

Answers on page 61.

PIX
FROM THE PACK:

THINK
THEREFORE
I PLAY

RUBEN
NEVES
MIDFIELDER

PIX

FROM THE PACK:

HERE COMES THE DENDONCKER

LEANDER
DENDONCKER

DEFENDER /MIDFIELDER

5 FOOT 7
OF FOOTBALL
HEAVEN

JOAO
MOUTINHO
MIDFIELDER

TRAINING DAYS

Time now for a bit of training fun, with some snaps from the work the lads took part in during the season.

The captions may not be entirely serious.

Look at this, boys – the no-look tying laces!

Here you are, Rui, let me tie yours as well.

Who took my drums away?

Conor, Conor – this is how you tie a lace.

I've fallen for the old superglue trick again.

I knew I should have put this before I got out here.

You ain't seen me...right?

Smiling...what's he done no

No, Pedro, I don't need you to tie my lace thank you.

So you think you can tie la better than me, Joao?

Tonight, Simon,
I am going to be singing Si Senor.

Own up,
who put the superglue on this football?

Rui, do you remember that film...
Coneheads?

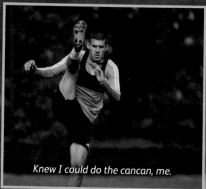
Knew I could do the cancan, me.

A Boly smile can always hide the guilt.

I caught one – it was this big!

He's smiling again.

Come on then – how does that dance go?

Did you know how good I am at the javelin?

Ruben, you know that superglue...

Agadoo, doo doo!

How do these things work again?

Let me do it, Rui, I know what
happens with this superglue.

Is it a bird? Is it a plane?

He's still smiling...

PIX

FROM THE PACK:

BACK OF THE NETO

PEDRO NETO
FORWARD

QUIZ:
WHO AM I?

Here is a quiz where you can test yourself against friends and family to see who knows most about the players who have represented Wolves since Nuno Espirito Santo took the helm in 2017.

For each question, there are five clues. If you guess the player straight away then it's five points, after two clues it's four, down to one point if it takes all five clues to identify the player. There are eight players, and all played for Nuno during his time at Molineux. Then at the end, add up your scores and see how many points you got out of 40. Remember, one clue at a time! Good luck! Answers on page 61.

1
CLUE 1: I joined Wolves at the age of 24.
CLUE 2: I had never played in England before joining Wolves.
CLUE 3: I made my debut in the opening game of the 2017/18 season against Middlesbrough.
CLUE 4: I wore squad number 33.
CLUE 5: At one point I scored nine goals in 11 games during the Championship-winning season.

2
CLUE 1: I have played international football for my country from Under-16 all the way to full internationals.
CLUE 2: I have captained Wolves.
CLUE 3: I am the youngest Portuguese player to feature in the Champions League.
CLUE 4: I have an ability to score spectacular long-range goals.
CLUE 5: I won three Wolves awards at the end of the 2017/18 season.

3
CLUE 1: I was involved in the first seven games of Nuno's time at Wolves.
CLUE 2: I came on as a substitute at Brentford in my last game for Wolves.
CLUE 3: I scored the first cup goal of Nuno's reign.
CLUE 4: I made 108 appearances for Wolves in total, scoring 35 goals.
CLUE 5: I was at the start of the famous song which was completed by 'Afobe, Sako.'

4
CLUE 1: I was born in 1996.
CLUE 2: Wolves are the third English club I have played for.
CLUE 3: I played against Wolves in their Championship-winning 2017/18 season.
CLUE 4: My first game in La Liga, I came off the bench to replace Neymar.
CLUE 5: I quite like providing assists for Raul Jimenez.

5
CLUE 1: I am a goalkeeper.
CLUE 2: I made my first senior appearance for Cambridge United.
CLUE 3: I was born in St Ives in Cambridgeshire.
CLUE 4: I was named in the PFA Team of the Year in the 2017/18 season.
CLUE 5: I saved an injury-time penalty when Wolves won at Cardiff in the Championship-winning season.

6
CLUE 1: Wolves were the first English club I joined.
CLUE 2: My first league appearance for Wolves came in the Premier League.
CLUE 3: I used to work for my dad's carpet-cleaning business.
CLUE 4: I scored my first goal for Wolves against Nottingham Forest.
CLUE 5: I scored the winning goal in our 3-2 win against Manchester City in the 2019/20 season.

7
CLUE 1: I had played in Spain before I moved to England.
CLUE 2: I came off the bench to make my Wolves debut against Millwall.
CLUE 3: My first Wolves goal was a winner against Barnsley.
CLUE 4: I have also played for Hull and Sunderland.
CLUE 5: I made two appearances for Senegal at the 2018 World Cup.

8
CLUE 1: I have played in several different positions for Wolves.
CLUE 2: I arrived initially on loan with the deal later becoming permanent.
CLUE 3: I made my league debut for Wolves against Chelsea.
CLUE 4: I scored my first goal for Wolves against Everton.
CLUE 5: I spent the first few years of my career with Anderlecht.

HOW DID YOU DO?

0-10 POINTS
Oh dear! Are you even a Wolves fan at all?

11-20 POINTS
Not the worst but not the best. Plenty of room for improvement.

21-30 POINTS
Solid performance – your Wolves player knowledge is up to scratch.

31-40 POINTS
Top identification skills! Would make a good police officer!

TEN TRAORE TEASERS

Pace, power, poise, potential - there aren't too many who play football like Adama Traore.

The jet-heeled pocket rocket of a Wolves winger has got the whole football world talking in recent years, such is his exhilarating threat running at opposition defenders and his development under Nuno Espirito Santo.

Here, the Wolves Annual takes a look at some facts and figures around the Spanish-born frontman - ten Traore teasers if you like. We take a look back at some of the news surrounding his career before joining Wolves, and then some of the statistics from his exciting 2019/20 season.

1 - BROUGHT UP AT BARCA

Having joined Barcelona's youth set-up at the age of just eight, Traore progressed to the 'B' team of the world giants. And then, in November 2013, he made his La Liga debut as a 17-year-old, coming off the bench to replace... none other than Neymar!

That team also included the likes of Pique, Fabregas, Iniesta, Busquets and Sanchez – no biggie! – but that was to prove Traore's only league appearance in a handful of overall outings for Barca.

2 - PULLED THROUGH BY PULIS

Traore had a difficult time at Aston Villa after moving from Barcelona, but help, and the rebuilding of his career, came from what might appear an unlikely source.

Tony Pulis has crafted an excellent managerial reputation on a no-nonsense traditional form of leadership, and it was he who took a keen interest in Traore after taking the helm at Middlesbrough, the club the winger moved to from Villa. In the six months they worked together, Pulis transformed Traore's game and especially his confidence.

"I cannot speak higher of a player I've ever worked with," said Pulis. *"He is a wonderful human being."*

3 - SLOWED DOWN BY A SPRINTER

Another factor behind Traore's resurgence on the Riverside was thanks to Olympic relay gold medallist sprinter Darren Campbell.

Campbell was called in to work with Traore at Middlesbrough, and actually encouraged him to slow himself down in order to make the right decision at the end of his blistering runs.

"In your car, you have six gears – Adama always used sixth gear," said Campbell. *"So, for me, the key straight away was slowing him down."*

4 - SEE YOU SOON, BOYS!

At the end of March 2018, Traore actually lined up against Wolves in a memorable game in which Ruben Neves and Matt Doherty were sent off, but Wolves clung on to win 2-1. He wouldn't have known it at the time, but, as he gazed over at Wolves' pre-match huddle, within five months he would be sharing the same dressing room as those involved rather than being in the opposition one. And back in the Premier League!

5 - RECORD-BREAKER

When Traore did check in at Molineux in the summer of 2018, it was for a club record fee, as Wolves met the £18 million release clause in his Middlesbrough contract. *"This is a great move for me and I am so happy,"* he said at the time. His first Molineux campaign may have been something of a transition and certainly not as explosive as his second, but a full pre-season with Nuno clearly reaped its rewards ahead of 2019/20.

A QUICK GLANCE THROUGH TRAORE'S STATS DURING THE 2019/20 SEASON:

6 - THE GOALS

Traore notched six goals in all competitions, but saved his Premier League ones for the big boys.

Namely Manchester City, grabbing both goals in the memorable win at the Etihad, followed by another in the equally memorable follow-up at Molineux, and another belter at home to Tottenham.

7 - THE ASSISTS

Traore improved his goal tally from one to six between his first and second Wolves seasons, but it was the improvement in quality of his crossing and decision-making which proved a particular highlight.

In total, he produced 12 assists during the Premier League season, and forged an extremely fruitful alliance with Raul Jimenez, their combinations leading to no fewer than 10 Wolves goals.

8 - THE SHOTS

Another area where Traore made great strides during the season came with getting himself into shooting positions, and then having a go!

His brace at Manchester City was based around breaking through and finishing calmly, but his goals at home to City and Tottenham were the result of powerful and unstoppable finishing.

All in all, Traore hit 75 shots during the 2019/20 Premier League campaign of which 21 were on target, an accuracy rating of 28%.

9 - THE BOOKINGS

The single-minded attitude and blistering speed in taking people on also secured Traore plenty of attention from the opposition, not least the Bournemouth player heard to scream 'Foul him' when it was easier to pick up sound after games moved behind closed doors.

One of the most fouled players in the Premier League, all in all a total of 34 opposition players received a yellow card for infringements against Traore during the season.

10 - THE LANDMARKS

During the 2019/20 season Traore made his 50th competitive appearance for Wolves, and marked it in some style.

It was the 2-0 away win at Manchester City, in which he clinically dispatched both goals, where he arrived at his half-century.

His 100th Premier League appearance for all clubs wasn't quite as eventful as he wasn't needed to deliver the same explosive impact, coming off the bench in the closing stages of the comfortable 3-0 home win against Everton.

Here's to many more landmarks to come!

43

PIX

DAN'S THE MAN!

DANIEL
PODENCE

FORWARD

PIX

FROM THE PACK:

A WHO JOT LOVE

DIOGO
JOTA
FORWARD

Following similar articles in previous editions of the Wolves Annual, here we catch up with another Wolves fan to find out more about their career in football.

Alex Gage is a broadcast cameraman with over 20 years' experience with Sky Sports, and in more recent times also films the current crop of Wolves talent by covering home games at Molineux for Wolves TV.

LIFE BEHIND THE LENS

FIRST OF ALL, ALEX, WE HAVE SEEN A PHOTO OF A VERY YOUNG 'YOU' WITH WOLVES HEROES OF THE 1970'S AND 80'S. HOW DID YOU BECOME A WOLVES FAN?

AG: My dad was a Londoner and a Spurs fan, but we moved to the Midlands when I was very young and he took me to Molineux a lot. I used to stand at the front of the South Bank or sit on the concrete wall with all the other kids, then meet him at half time for a pie. He worked in newspaper sales, and that photo was taken at Molineux when there was some kind of newspaper competition to win a BMX bike. I am not sure how I ended up in the background!

AS YOU GREW OLDER, HOW DID YOU GET INVOLVED IN WORKING AS A CAMERAMAN?

AG: I started at Birmingham L!VE TV, a cable-TV channel in Birmingham, as a runner, which basically means carrying out lots of basic tasks for the producer and staff. I certainly learnt how to make a good cup of tea but also listened to cameramen who taught me on the job. From there, I moved to Boro TV, the first club TV channel in the country, at Middlesbrough FC (which launched shortly before MUTV). After a year or so there, a cameraman approached me and offered me a contract with Sky Sports in Sheffield. That's how it all began.

SO WHAT DOES WORK INVOLVE NOW?

AG: My job now as a freelance cameraman has a wide range of work, or at least it did before Covid! The best thing about the job is the variety; it could be a press conference, an interview abroad, a fishing competition, a football match, or filming a horse on the gallops. Every day is different and I wouldn't ever want to change that.

FOR ALL THE GREAT EVENTS YOU GET TO COVER, IT'S NOT ALL GLAMOUR IS IT?

AG: Transfer deadline day comes around in football twice a year, and one of them is always in January. Which is all very exciting if you're sat at home watching it on telly. But spare a thought for the poor cameramen and reporters, sat outside the training grounds all day, from 5.30 in the morning often until midnight, waiting for the famous (or not so famous!) players to arrive... who more often than not turn out to just be a rumour anyway!

WHAT IS IT LIKE WORKING WITH PLAYERS AND MANAGERS?

AG: More often than not, it's an absolute pleasure. The people you've only ever seen on the pitch or on telly usually turn out to be really nice and interesting. A lot of them are very funny, and they're often interested in the camera, and how they're going to look when it goes out on screen! Of the current Wolves squad, Conor Coady and Romain Saiss are particularly funny guys - they've always got a joke ready to tell.

ANY PARTICULARLY FUNNY MOMENTS WHILE FILMING?

AG: Well yes, quite a few. People of a certain age might remember Stuart McCall celebrating Bradford's promotion by falling off a car on the night after they had won at Wolves to reach the Premier League. That was my footage. On another occasion, I was sent to Neil Warnock's house to set him up in front of the camera for a live interview with someone in the Sky studio. I was younger, and more naïve, so when someone who turned out to be an electrician sent me upstairs to find him, all of a sudden I walked into a room and Neil and his wife were sat up eating their morning toast in bed! I think he saw the funny side but very firmly suggested we did the filming downstairs. Walking or running backwards to get the right shot

can be tricky. I once took a proper tumble filming Ian Wright on his first appearance for Burnley, which he (and the crowd!) seemed to enjoy.

The game had finished 0-0, and me falling over got the biggest cheer of the afternoon. Another time, I was filming in Mark McGhee's garden when he was at Wolves and ended up falling in his pond. Good times!

ANY PARTICULARLY GREAT MOMENTS YOU CAN REMEMBER FROM FILMING?

AG: In 2004, I filmed a Champions League game between Real Madrid and Bayern Munich at the Bernabeu Stadium in Madrid. Zinedine Zidane scored the only goal, and I'll never forget his face as he ran shouting straight towards me. It was amazing, and for a moment felt like we were the only two people in the stadium.

Wolves-wise, Ruben Neves' goal against Derby takes some beating. I was on the side of the pitch, in line with him as he trapped it. As it bounced into the air, you could see what was coming next, though you couldn't really believe he'd try it. I followed the ball in slow motion, all the way past Scott Carson's despairing dive and into the net, then whipped the camera back to catch Ruben charging off in celebration. What a goal!

AND THE OPPOSITE. ANY HARD-LUCK STORIES?

AG: It doesn't happen often, but when the camera fails it can leave you high and dry. When Matt Doherty scored the winner against Man City, I had an excited text from Yannie, who's the boss of the brilliant video team at Wolves, saying 'that's going to look amazing!' I had to text him back and explain that my camera had frozen 30 seconds beforehand and I was in the middle of that old trick, turning it off and on again, as Matt broke through and scored. Heart-breaking for me, but we had it covered from plenty of other angles, so it turned out OK for our coverage.

WHAT IS THE BEST ADVICE YOU HAVE EVER BEEN GIVEN?

AG: The best advice I've ever been given was that in a job like mine it's 10 per cent your skill with the camera and 90 per cent your skill at getting on with people. And if your last shot is no good, make sure your next shot is brilliant.

FINALLY, WHAT ADVICE WOULD YOU GIVE SOMEONE LOOKING TO GET INTO FOOTBALL MEDIA?

AG: I'd tell anyone who wants to get into filming football to watch plenty of football! That will give you an idea of the shots that look good, and the shots that don't work so well. Then go to your local football team and ask if anyone films the games. If they don't, offer to do it. Maybe cut the highlights together and put it on YouTube. You'll be amazed how much better you get at it as the season goes on. But, mainly, never stop enjoying the football!

WOLFIE'S FUN PAGE

Con-crest!

We've merged the Wolves crest with those of two other 20/21 Premier League clubs – do you know which?

Spot the Difference

Can you find the six differences between these two pictures?

The A-maze-ing Game!

Can you guide Wolfie's football into the back of the net?

START

GOAL!

Did you know?

The world record for spinning a basketball on one finger using one hand is over 11 minutes! How long can you spin a football?

Did you know?

An estimated 715.1 million people (a ninth of the entire population of the planet) tuned in to watch the 2006 World Cup Final!

Sil-who-ette?

Which speedy Wolves player is hidden in the shadow?

COLOUR ME IN!

RAÚL JIMÉNEZ

Howlers...

Which sports players are the warmest in the winter?

Long jumpers!

Hidden Words

Six words have been hidden in the grid. They are all to do with items players wear on the pitch. Can you find them all?

W	N	A	I					
G	Y	B	X					
L	J	T	U					
O	S	S	Z					
V	H	C	H					
E	O	Q	A	I	S	O	C	K	S
S	R	L	V	P	R	K	E	G	R
D	T	H	B	O	O	T	S	S	F
O	S	H	I	N	P	A	D	S	M

Scrambled Shirts

The letters have been mixed up on these shirts. Can you figure out which players they belong to?

COPNEED

NKNDECODER

Answers on page 61.

Young Wolves

LIKE EVERYONE, YOUNG WOLVES HAD A VERY DIFFERENT AND INTERRUPTED SEASON DUE TO THE COVID-19 PANDEMIC, BUT THERE WAS STILL PLENTY OF FUN TO BE HAD BEFORE LOCKDOWN TOOK HOLD.

Once again, the mascot packages proved extremely popular for league and cup games, as well as welcoming local primary-school children to be player escorts for the home Europa League fixtures.

The Junior Christmas events were another big highlight, featuring two movie nights at the Light House Cinema and the Dribblers party at Molineux.

Special guests included Chairman Jeff Shi, Vice-President Steve Bull and players including Morgan Gibbs-White and Bruno Jordao.

Prior to that came the always popular open training session, with the chance to watch the team at close quarters and take part in games and activities.

Young Wolves were then looking forward to reuniting with the club's fans and hopefully being part of more fantastic events during the 2020/21 season. (Turn over for all the membership details for the 2020/21 campaign.)

Official Wolves
MEMBERSHIPS
SEASON 2020/21

My Wolves
ADULT - 17+

Membership includes:

- Exclusive joining gifts (Hat, lucky socks & pin badge)
- Smartcard
- Ability to earn Wolves Cash on tickets and merchandise (10% of spend)
- 100 Loyalty Points
- Ability to join season-ticket waiting list
- Invitations to exclusive members-only events

£35.00* for the season *Excluding P&P

Wolf Pack
AGES 12-16

Membership includes:

- Exclusive joining gifts (Earbuds & phone accessory)
- Smartcard
- Ability to earn Wolves Cash on tickets and merchandise (10% of spend)
- 100 Loyalty Points
- Ability to join season-ticket waiting list
- Invitations to exclusive members-only events

£20.00* for the season *Excluding P&P

Young Wolves
AGES 3-11

Membership includes:

- Exclusive joining gifts (Colour-in ball & flag)
- Smartcard
- Ability to earn Wolves Cash on tickets and merchandise (10% of spend)
- 100 Loyalty Points
- Ability to join season-ticket waiting list
- Invitations to exclusive members-only events

£20.00* for the season *Excluding P&P

Wolves Dribblers
AGES 0-2

Membership includes:

- Exclusive joining gift (Comfort blanket in a keepsake box)
- Ability to earn Wolves Cash on tickets and merchandise (10% of spend)
- Smartcard
- Certificate from Nuno
- Invitations to exclusive members-only events

£15.00* for the season *Excluding P&P

NOW IS THE TIME

TO PURCHASE YOUR MEMBERSHIP FOR THE 2020/21 SEASON

NEW FOR 2020/21 SEASON:

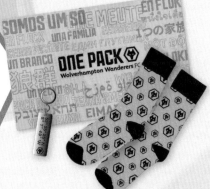

International Membership
ADULT- 17+

Membership includes:

- Exclusive joining gifts (Lucky socks, keyring and international flag)
- Priority access to tickets (option to buy tickets at MyWolves window stage)
- Museum entrance voucher
- 1 x voucher for free shipping at shop.wolves.co.uk
- Access to Worldwide Wolves Lounge on matchday
  (membership card or a ST will be a compulsory requirement for lounge access from 20/21)
- Membership smartcard (ability to earn and redeem Wolves Cash on all ticket and retail purchases)
- Invitations to exclusive members-only events

INTRODUCTORY PRICE: £35.00 plus postage

Join online at **tickets.wolves.co.uk** or
via the ticket office on **0371 222 1877**.

WOLVES WOMEN: A UNIQUE SEASON

The 2019/20 campaign was something of a bittersweet one for Wolves Women.

'Sweet' in that the team produced such a fantastic seven months of action to be sitting nine points clear at the top of Division 1 Midlands of the National League with seven games remaining when the Covid-19 pandemic arrived.

And 'bitter', or perhaps more accurately extremely frustrating and disappointing, that while it was totally understandable that the season came to a halt, the FA decided that tiers three to seven of women's football would come to an immediate end with no promotion or relegation.

But 14 league wins and just one defeat is a record which the team should be very proud of, and hopefully lays a strong foundation to go out and do it all again in the 2020/21 season. We caught up with head coach Dan McNamara, to look back at some of the best moments from the season.

BEST LEADER

I can comfortably say Anna Price for this one. To have spent over 25 years at one club is an incredible achievement for anyone and what Anna brings is absolutely outstanding leadership. And when Anna was missing another long-serving member of the team Natalie Widdal was really important. Widds made her 200th appearance during the season and was another player who was fantastic for us on and off the pitch.

Captain, leader, legend – Anna Price!

BEST BREAKTHROUGH

We had a few who broke through during the season. I'd go with Nyah Edwards and Katie Johnson from the RTC (Regional Talent Centre) if I had to name a couple. They both made great progress and really improved as the year went on, both being rewarded by getting a number of appearances in the first team.

BEST MUSIC

I'll probably not get too involved in this one. There are a mixture of musical tastes in the dressing room and a lot of the girls are often vying to control the speaker! Jam is one of them, Widds is another, and it's a lot of rap music nowadays! And then we play the Wolves song as we walk out. One of our coaching staff Marcus isn't a huge fan of the pre-match music and is always keen to get some Spanish stuff on there instead!

BEST PLAYER

The Players' Player of the Season award went to Jamila Palmer. Jam was fantastic and was often the key difference in games. She has got real quality and can produce moments of brilliance.

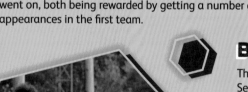

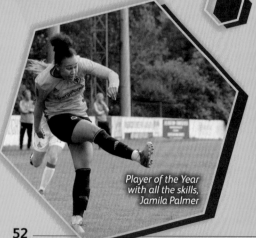

Player of the Year with all the skills, Jamila Palmer

BEST SKILLS

Sorry but it's Jam again! And that's something the girls have said themselves, so I'm happy to go along with that.

BEST MATCH

One of the big highlights was our game away at Fylde – who are a league above us – in the League Cup. We were 2-1 down with three minutes of extra time remaining and we won 3-2. That was a standout game. And the TNS game at home, after we had lost away, was a big moment as well. Winning that game 5-1 was the first time we probably felt we had one hand on the trophy.

BEST MOMENT

We had gone up to Doncaster Belles, which turned out to be the last Sunday before lockdown. We knew if we won that game we had the chance to win the league in the following game against Sporting Khalsa which was going to be at Molineux. When that final whistle went at Donny, and we had won 1-0 thanks to Sophie Bramford's goal, it was such a relief and a great moment because we felt we were so close to achieving it. Sadly it wasn't to be in the end.

FUNNIEST MOMENT

That probably came in the celebrations at the Fylde game I have already mentioned when Anna Morphet scored a free kick and the whole of the coaching staff ran down the line to celebrate with the girls. Our psychologist Nick Hitchman ended up with a bloody nose after coming up from the melee after such a wild celebration. We all found it funny anyway – I'm sure Nick won't mind!

BEST BANTER

Another very similar answer here I'm afraid. Jam is very much the comedienne of the group who is often at the forefront of the jokes. Widds is also very jovial. And then this year we have got Tammi George coming back in and rejoining us from Spurs. She likes to wind people up so seeing how those three bring the dressing room together will be interesting!

BEST TACKLER

Shannie Jennings. She gets booked every week. She loves flying in for a challenge. Widds is another who loves a tackle. Sometimes we think she has a poor first touch just so it gives her the chance to fly into a tackle.

Shannie Jennings takes no prisoners!

Natalie Widdal, a key figure on and off the pitch

MACCA'S MESSAGE

It was so disappointing the way it all ended after what had been such a good season. But I want to say from myself, all the staff and all the players, just a huge thank you to everyone at the club for all that they did for us. It has been amazing to see Jeff Shi say that he wants to support us further and that we only have to ask for anything else that we need. It's very much a 'watch this space' now with people questioning our mentality and whether we can come back from feeling rock bottom and go and do it all again. With the group of girls that we have, and the signings that we have added, I think the mentality will be as good as ever and we are looking forward to the challenges ahead.

Another goal celebrated by the Wolves Women

MEMORY MATCH

May 22nd, 2021, will mark the tenth anniversary of one of the most memorable afternoons at Molineux in recent history. The day Wolves lost a crucial relegation decider against Blackburn - but still won by staying up.

Here we take a look back at the final day of the 2010/11 Premier League season, almost a decade on.

Karl Henry leads Wolves out ahead of a nerve-jangling final day in the Premier League. West Ham were already relegated, but Wolves started the day as one of five teams separated by just a single point in the race to avoid being one of the two others joining the Hammers.

Huddle time before kick-off. Starting the day in 16th, what was even more intriguing was that Wolves' visitors Blackburn, just a place above and ahead of Wolves only on goal difference, were also under threat. Birmingham, Blackpool and Wigan were all a point adrift on 39, just below Wolves. Those four are also separated by only three goals when it comes to goal difference.

A crowd of 29,009 is packed into Molineux and the early stages are very tense with skipper Karl Henry landing an early booking. "I can't put into words how big this game is," Henry had said before the match. Both sides are working their way into the game in the early stages and there are no key goals elsewhere either.

Disaster for Wolves. Midway through the first half Jason Roberts puts Blackburn in front. For now though Wolves are OK, as Blackpool have gone behind at Manchester United and, at present, are going down with Wigan, who are drawing at Stoke.

It gets worse very quickly for Wolves, and Mick McCarthy is understandably growing in annoyance. Two more goals are conceded before half time, to Brett Emerton and Junior Hoilett. As it stands Wolves are down, joining fellow W's Wigan and West Ham, with Blackburn, Blackpool, back level with Manchester United, and Birmingham, goalless at Spurs, the survivors.

Sylvan Ebanks-Blake was sent on at half time to try to help Wolves somehow get back into the game. A goal from Roman Pavlyuchenko for Spurs against Birmingham puts the Blues into the relegation zone and, for now, Wolves are safe. Blackpool temporarily lead at Old Trafford before United hit back to equalise.

54

A FLURRY OF GOALS AT THE BOTTOM, INCLUDING, AT LAST, ONE FOR WOLVES, AS JAMIE O'HARA FIRES HOME. BLACKPOOL QUICKLY CONCEDE TWICE TO GO 4-2 DOWN AT MANCHESTER UNITED – THEY ARE GONE. BUT BIRMINGHAM DRAW LEVEL AT SPURS, AND WIGAN TAKE THE LEAD AT STOKE. SO WOLVES, BY VIRTUE OF BEING ONE GOAL WORSE OFF TO THEIR MIDLANDS RIVALS, ARE CURRENTLY GOING DOWN.

"WE ONLY NEED ONE GOAL," SCREAM THE RIDICULOUSLY NERVOUS MOLINEUX FAITHFUL. SO THEY DO, BECAUSE A GOAL WOULD TAKE WOLVES LEVEL ON GOAL DIFFERENCE WITH BIRMINGHAM IF THEY TAKE A POINT, BUT AHEAD ON GOALS SCORED. AND THEN, DELICIOUSLY, ON 87 MINUTES, THE GOAL ARRIVES, STEPHEN HUNT CURLING A SUPERB EFFORT INTO THE TOP CORNER. CUE PANDEMONIUM.

STILL, THOUGH, JUST ONE BIRMINGHAM GOAL WOULD SEND WOLVES DOWN. AND YET, HUNT'S SPECTACULAR STRIKE HAS CHANGED EVERYTHING. BECAUSE IT PUSHES BLUES FORWARD IN SEARCH OF THAT GOAL, AND SPURS BREAK, ALLOWING PAVLYUCHENKO TO SLAM HOME HIS SECOND. NOT LONG AFTER, THE FINAL WHISTLE SOUNDS AT MOLINEUX AND MICK MCCARTHY EXCHANGES PLEASANTRIES WITH BLACKBURN COUNTERPART STEVE KEAN.

SOME PEOPLE ARE ON THE PITCH, THEY THINK IT'S ALL OVER. AND INDEED IT IS. SOMEHOW WOLVES HAVE LOST, BUT STILL SURVIVED, AND THAT HUNT GOAL WAS THE CRUCIAL CATALYST. A MIXTURE OF RELIEF AND EXCITEMENT AS FANS PILE ONTO THE PITCH.

"YOU'VE LET US DOWN AGAIN" WAS THE STARK MESSAGE FROM A COUPLE OF WOLVES FANS AFTER ONE OF THE MANY DOSES OF PLAY-OFF MISERY NINE YEARS EARLIER. THIS TIME AROUND, THIS LATEST IN THE FAMOUS 'TOASTER' SERIES SUMMED IT UP PERFECTLY.

A GREAT MOMENT OF CELEBRATION OR PERHAPS CONTEMPLATION FOR MCCARTHY AND HIS ASSISTANT TERRY CONNOR, WHO WAS CREDITED WITH A PARTICULARLY POWERFUL HALF-TIME ADDRESS TO BOOST THE PLAYERS AFTER SUCH AN HORRENDOUS FIRST HALF.

CELEBRATIONS WERE MORE ROWDY IN THE DRESSING ROOM AS RICHARD STEARMAN, STEPHEN WARD AND WAYNE HENNESSEY WERE AMONGST PLAYERS SALUTING SURVIVAL, ECHOING SCENES OF THEIR CHAMPIONSHIP TITLE SUCCESS FROM TWO YEARS PREVIOUSLY, BUT THIS TIME IN VERY DIFFERENT CIRCUMSTANCES.

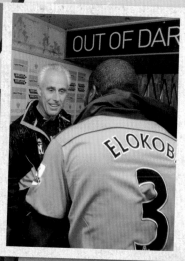

"NEVER IN DOUBT"

JOKED MICK MCCARTHY, BEFORE ADMITTING HE WAS "MIGHTILY RELIEVED" IN HIS POST-MATCH INTERVIEW. FOLLOWED BY THE INTERRUPTION AS GEORGE ELOKOBI ARRIVED WITH CHAMPAGNE IN TOW! "IF IT WASN'T ELOKOBI, I'D DO HIM," RESPONDED THE BOSS! A SURREAL END TO A SURREAL AFTERNOON!

THE ★ AMERICAN ★ DREAM

Kevin Foley and Neill Collins were both part of Wolves' Championship-winning season back in 2008/09, and Foley was involved in the Blackburn game featured on the previous pages. Collins was appointed manager of Tampa Bay Rowdies back in 2018 and, early in 2020, Foley became one of the club's assistant coaches as the defenders linked up again in the USA.

The Wolves Annual caught up with Kevin to find out more.

So, Kevin, it was all the way back in 2007 you joined Wolves. What can you remember of that time?

KF: I had played against Wolves twice for Luton the season before and managed to play well. Mick McCarthy said when I signed that my performances had stood out for him.
Going on to get to know him as I did through the years that was something that he did quite often – he would take notice of people who played well against his teams and trust his own eye. Maybe it helped that I was Irish as well... Mick did sign a fair few Irish lads at that time!
I have to say I didn't realise how big a club Wolves was until I first came for talks. I just thought it was amazing the first time I walked through the door and it was the easiest decision I could ever have made.

What was it like at Wolves during that spell under Mick?

KF: I would have to say Mick was the best manager I worked for. It is when I played my best football, and so I think that follows. He got the best out of me, and I think he gets the best out of all of his players. He builds teams of good characters, and if you are not a good character, you don't play for him. You can never really relax if you are playing for Mick and that is a good thing – it keeps you on your toes. The dressing room was fantastic and there was some great banter – quite vicious, but funny. And it made everyone stronger. A lot of us had come from lower teams, and we were so desperate for success.

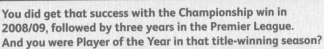

You did get that success with the Championship win in 2008/09, followed by three years in the Premier League. And you were Player of the Year in that title-winning season?

KF: Getting that award from the fans was such an honour for me. I was playing at right back, and Sylvan (Ebanks-Blake) was banging the goals in and Lumes (Chris Iwelumo) and Kights (Michael Kightly). To reach the Premier League was always the aim, but it was the icing on the cake and a really proud moment for me to get the award. It was nice to be recognised and it was definitely the best football I played in my career.

Your career carried on after leaving Wolves before coming to an end. Was coaching always in your thoughts?

KF: When I was playing I never really had a plan in my head of what I was going to do or what I wanted to do. But I knew that for many, the natural progression for a footballer was to dip your toe into coaching. While I was playing, I took the opportunity to complete my 'A' and 'B' licences through the Football Association of Ireland, so when I finished I wasn't scrambling around trying to get organised. I had always kept a good relationship with Wolves and spoke to Kevin Thelwell and Scott Sellars, and Rob Edwards who was coaching there at the time, and came in for a couple of weeks to observe training and look behind the scenes at everything that was going on. Before I knew it I had an opportunity to work in the Academy and help those young and aspiring footballers in any way that I could.

And you then moved on to coaching one of the age groups?

KF: Yes, I was in charge of the Under-13s, which was a great opportunity and also a big responsibility. Choosing a team, picking the tactics, seeing how the games worked. In many ways it is a lot harder coaching a young player than a more experienced player. It is like being a schoolteacher, doing reviews, talking to parents, and it really opened my eyes to what is now involved in Academy football. It wasn't like that when I was coming through at Luton. We trained on a Tuesday and a Thursday night, and the coaches were great, but there was no day release off school or all the other support young players get now. They learn so much more than just what happens on the pitch – they are so much more tactically aware and ask some great questions.

So you were coaching at Wolves Academy and then, all of a sudden, a certain former Wolves team-mate got in touch?

KF: Yes. Neill Collins is a good friend of mine from our time at Wolves and he is now manager of the Tampa Bay Rowdies in the United Soccer League in America. He called me towards the end of 2019 as he was looking to add another coach to the team. A week later, me and my wife flew out there to meet Neill and look at the club and some houses and schools. We both felt we would be stupid not to go for this opportunity. In football you are never quite sure when you might get a chance like this at a professional level and I would have kicked myself if I hadn't taken it on. In Florida of all places! It was a no-brainer for us really. The pandemic arrived not long after we had come out here and it's been very difficult for everyone, but we have been very fortunate that we have been in a place like Florida during lockdown.

The USL season got going again after the pandemic. How have you found the coaching side of it all?

KF: The players out here are so receptive. It's not the Premier League, but the boys out here have still got aspirations to get to the MLS (Major League Soccer) or to try and go and play in Europe. Their work ethic is outstanding, which I think comes from their make-up in terms of America and the college system, where if you are not working hard, you don't get on the team. Sometimes they can try too hard, and you have to tell them to relax a little bit and not be too hard on themselves. It's a great attribute to have though and coaching players like that is a dream.

How has it been linking up with Neill again, having previously played alongside him?

KF: Neill wears his heart on his sleeve but is also a calm guy as a coach. Every good coach gets respect from the players and Neill has that at Tampa, and he also played in the team with many of them before he got the job. I think he wanted to hire me because I am different to him, maybe he thinks I am a little bit calmer, but it is certainly good to have different personalities. We have got another young coach here in Chad Burt who used to play for the Rowdies and we've probably got one of the youngest set-ups in the USL. It's working well, and we've all been professional players and can relate to the lads here, which is a real positive.

How are you finding the tension of matchdays on the sidelines?

KF: To be honest I think I was a bit too relaxed! Then I started to think I needed to drink a few Red Bulls to get me going! All our games are in the evenings so we have to wait through the day and I am still in that learning phase. When the game starts, I am looking at how the opposition are playing, whether we need to adjust tactically, what we can do to improve things on the pitch. I am really enjoying it, planning set pieces, looking at tactics, building working relationships with the players. Everyone is different, and it is good to learn what it takes to get the most out of each individual player.

How have you and the Foley family settled in off the pitch?

KF: We're all enjoying it. The kids started at school and were getting on really well, then the lockdown came. It would have been great for them to meet more people and get into all the soccer clubs, but that will come. People over here are very friendly and my wife Llewella has also adjusted really well.

Finally then, after all your time at Wolves, if someone had said a few years later you and Neill would be involved in this new footballing adventure, would you have believed them?

KF: Probably not! Neill was always banging on about doing his badges and getting into coaching when he was a player, but who would have thought it eh? It's incredible, and who knows what the future holds. I am just focused on doing as well as I can in the job I am in and taking it from there. I am really grateful to have this opportunity and really glad that I have taken it on.

PIX

FROM THE PACK:

¡SI SEÑOR!

RAÚL
JIMÉNEZ
STRIKER

WOLVES
OFFICIAL
2020/21
HOME KIT

**BUY NOW IN STORE AND ONLINE
AT SHOP.WOLVES.CO.UK**